Welcome & Thank you

Congratulations

Self Care is important and you have taken a step forward by purchasing this workbook. I commend you for understanding how important your well being is. You have made yourself a priority. Doing so not only benefits you, but the people you love as well. The peopple who love you and depnd on you would much rather see you positive, full of energy and happy, than tired, unhappy and emotionally drainged.

This self care workbook will help to equip you with the knowledge and tools to make self care an ongoing part of your life's journey.

Thank you for choosing our workbook to assist you with your journey

Moreen Jordan, M.A., L.P.C.
Marital & Family Therapist

Copyright @ 2021 by Moreen Jordan, M.A., L.P.C.
www.moreenjordan.com

ISBN: (paperback)
978-1-7373521-4-3

Printed in the United States of American

First Edition 2021
First Printing 2021

Moreen Jordan is a licensed mental health professional, Christian counselor, Speaker, Trainer and Consultant specializing in working with individuals, couples, families and corporations who have experienced trauma and/or witnessed traumatic events. She has worked with First responders and Military personnel both nationally and internationally. She is the President/CEO of Aspiring Life Change Counseling & Consulting, LLC And Compassion and Grace Counseling & Consulting (a non-profit organization).

Moreen empowers individuals and couples to overcome personal obstacles so that they can once again live purposeful and joy filled lives while honoring their past. Having overcome her own life-altering trauma, it has given her the passion to reach out to others and support them in their healing process. Moreen's own life is living proof of one's ability to overcome life's obstacles and she is determined to help others to reclaim their purpose, power and confidence.

She has her Master of Arts in Marital & Family Therapy and is a Licensed Professional Counselor. She is also a Certified Trauma Professional and Critical Incident Stress Debriefer (CISD) and has over 25+ years of counseling and behavioral health experience.

If you would like to contact her for a speaking engagement, training or other services please contact her at moreenthetherapist@gmail.com

This Book Belongs To:

Daily Journal

I am Grateful for

The Best thing about Today

Things I learned today!

Goals for the day

Action steps to meet goal(s)

Thoughts & Reflections of the day

Daily Journal

I am Grateful for

The Best thing about Today

Things I learned today!

Goals for the day

Action steps to meet goal(s)

Thoughts & Reflections of the day

Daily Journal

I am Grateful for

The Best thing about Today

Things I learned today!

Goals for the day

Action steps to meet goal(s)

Thoughts & Reflections of the day

Daily Journal

I am Grateful for

The Best thing about Today

Things I learned today!

Goals for the day

Action steps to meet goal(s)

Thoughts & Reflections of the day

Daily Journal

I am Grateful for

The Best thing about Today

Things I learned today!

Goals for the day

Action steps to meet goal(s)

Thoughts & Reflections of the day

Daily Journal

I am Grateful for

The Best thing about Today

Things I learned today!

Goals for the day

Action steps to meet goal(s)

Thoughts & Reflections of the day

Daily Journal

I am Grateful for	The Best thing about Today

Things I learned today!

Goals for the day	Action steps to meet goal(s)

Thoughts & Reflections of the day

Daily Journal

I am Grateful for

The Best thing about Today

Things I learned today!

Goals for the day

Action steps to meet goal(s)

Thoughts & Reflections of the day

Daily Journal

I am Grateful for

The Best thing about Today

Things I learned today!

Goals for the day

Action steps to meet goal(s)

Thoughts & Reflections of the day

Daily Journal

I am Grateful for	The Best thing about Today

Things I learned today!

Goals for the day	Action steps to meet goal(s)

Thoughts & Reflections of the day

Daily Journal

I am Grateful for

The Best thing about Today

Things I learned today!

Goals for the day

Action steps to meet goal(s)

Thoughts & Reflections of the day

Daily Journal

I am Grateful for

The Best thing about Today

Things I learned today!

Goals for the day

Action steps to meet goal(s)

Thoughts & Reflections of the day

Daily Journal

I am Grateful for

The Best thing about Today

Things I learned today!

Goals for the day

Action steps to meet goal(s)

Thoughts & Reflections of the day

Daily Journal

I am Grateful for

The Best thing about Today

Things I learned today!

Goals for the day

Action steps to meet goal(s)

Thoughts & Reflections of the day

Daily Journal

I am Grateful for

The Best thing about Today

Things I learned today!

Goals for the day

Action steps to meet goal(s)

Thoughts & Reflections of the day

Daily Journal

I am Grateful for

The Best thing about Today

Things I learned today!

Goals for the day

Action steps to meet goal(s)

Thoughts & Reflections of the day

Daily Journal

I am Grateful for

The Best thing about Today

Things I learned today!

Goals for the day

Action steps to meet goal(s)

Thoughts & Reflections of the day

Daily Journal

I am Grateful for

The Best thing about Today

Things I learned today!

Goals for the day

Action steps to meet goal(s)

Thoughts & Reflections of the day

Daily Journal

I am Grateful for	The Best thing about Today

Things I learned today!

Goals for the day	Action steps to meet goal(s)

Thoughts & Reflections of the day

Daily Journal

I am Grateful for

The Best thing about Today

Things I learned today!

Goals for the day

Action steps to meet goal(s)

Thoughts & Reflections of the day

Daily Journal

I am Grateful for

The Best thing about Today

Things I learned today!

Goals for the day

Action steps to meet goal(s)

Thoughts & Reflections of the day

Daily Journal

I am Grateful for

The Best thing about Today

Things I learned today!

Goals for the day

Action steps to meet goal(s)

Thoughts & Reflections of the day

Daily Journal

I am Grateful for

The Best thing about Today

Things I learned today!

Goals for the day

Action steps to meet goal(s)

Thoughts & Reflections of the day

Daily Journal

I am Grateful for

The Best thing about Today

Things I learned today!

Goals for the day

Action steps to meet goal(s)

Thoughts & Reflections of the day

Daily Journal

I am Grateful for

The Best thing about Today

Things I learned today!

Goals for the day

Action steps to meet goal(s)

Thoughts & Reflections of the day

Daily Journal

I am Grateful for

The Best thing about Today

Things I learned today!

Goals for the day

Action steps to meet goal(s)

Thoughts & Reflections of the day

Daily Journal

I am Grateful for

The Best thing about Today

Things I learned today!

Goals for the day

Action steps to meet goal(s)

Thoughts & Reflections of the day

Daily Journal

I am Grateful for

The Best thing about Today

Things I learned today!

Goals for the day

Action steps to meet goal(s)

Thoughts & Reflections of the day

Daily Journal

I am Grateful for

The Best thing about Today

Things I learned today!

Goals for the day

Action steps to meet goal(s)

Thoughts & Reflections of the day

Daily Journal

I am Grateful for

The Best thing about Today

Things I learned today!

Goals for the day

Action steps to meet goal(s)

Thoughts & Reflections of the day

Daily Journal

I am Grateful for

The Best thing about Today

Things I learned today!

Goals for the day

Action steps to meet goal(s)

Thoughts & Reflections of the day

Daily Journal

I am Grateful for

The Best thing about Today

Things I learned today!

Goals for the day

Action steps to meet goal(s)

Thoughts & Reflections of the day

Daily Journal

Things I learned today!

Thoughts & Reflections of the day

Daily Journal

Things I learned today!

Thoughts & Reflections of the day

Daily Journal

I am Grateful for

The Best thing about Today

Things I learned today!

Goals for the day

Action steps to meet goal(s)

Thoughts & Reflections of the day

Daily Journal

I am Grateful for

The Best thing about Today

Things I learned today!

Goals for the day

Action steps to meet goal(s)

Thoughts & Reflections of the day

Daily Journal

I am Grateful for

The Best thing about Today

Things I learned today!

Goals for the day

Action steps to meet goal(s)

Thoughts & Reflections of the day

Daily Journal

I am Grateful for	The Best thing about Today

Things I learned today!

Goals for the day	Action steps to meet goal(s)

Thoughts & Reflections of the day

Daily Journal

Things I learned today!

Thoughts & Reflections of the day

Daily Journal

I am Grateful for

The Best thing about Today

Things I learned today!

Goals for the day

Action steps to meet goal(s)

Thoughts & Reflections of the day

Daily Journal

I am Grateful for

The Best thing about Today

Things I learned today!

Goals for the day

Action steps to meet goal(s)

Thoughts & Reflections of the day

Daily Journal

I am Grateful for

The Best thing about Today

Things I learned today!

Goals for the day

Action steps to meet goal(s)

Thoughts & Reflections of the day

Daily Journal

I am Grateful for

The Best thing about Today

Things I learned today!

Goals for the day

Action steps to meet goal(s)

Thoughts & Reflections of the day

Daily Journal

I am Grateful for

The Best thing about Today

Things I learned today!

Goals for the day

Action steps to meet goal(s)

Thoughts & Reflections of the day

Daily Journal

I am Grateful for

The Best thing about Today

Things I learned today!

Goals for the day

Action steps to meet goal(s)

Thoughts & Reflections of the day

Daily Journal

I am Grateful for

The Best thing about Today

Things I learned today!

Goals for the day

Action steps to meet goal(s)

Thoughts & Reflections of the day

Daily Journal

Things I learned today!

Daily Journal

I am Grateful for

The Best thing about Today

Things I learned today!

Goals for the day

Action steps to meet goal(s)

Thoughts & Reflections of the day

Daily Journal

I am Grateful for

The Best thing about Today

Things I learned today!

Goals for the day

Action steps to meet goal(s)

Thoughts & Reflections of the day

Daily Journal

I am Grateful for

The Best thing about Today

Things I learned today!

Goals for the day

Action steps to meet goal(s)

Thoughts & Reflections of the day

Daily Journal

I am Grateful for

The Best thing about Today

Things I learned today!

Goals for the day

Action steps to meet goal(s)

Thoughts & Reflections of the day

Daily Journal

I am Grateful for

The Best thing about Today

Things I learned today!

Goals for the day

Action steps to meet goal(s)

Thoughts & Reflections of the day

Daily Journal

I am Grateful for

The Best thing about Today

Things I learned today!

Goals for the day

Action steps to meet goal(s)

Thoughts & Reflections of the day

Daily Journal

I am Grateful for

The Best thing about Today

Things I learned today!

Goals for the day

Action steps to meet goal(s)

Thoughts & Reflections of the day

Daily Journal

| I am Grateful for | The Best thing about Today |

Things I learned today!

| Goals for the day | Action steps to meet goal(s) |

Thoughts & Reflections of the day

Daily Journal

I am Grateful for	The Best thing about Today

Things I learned today!

Goals for the day	Action steps to meet goal(s)

Thoughts & Reflections of the day

Daily Journal

<table>
<tr><td>I am Grateful for</td><td>The Best thing about Today</td></tr>
</table>

Things I learned today!

<table>
<tr><td>Goals for the day</td><td>Action steps to meet goal(s)</td></tr>
</table>

Thoughts & Reflections of the day

Daily Journal

I am Grateful for

The Best thing about Today

Things I learned today!

Goals for the day

Action steps to meet goal(s)

Thoughts & Reflections of the day

Daily Journal

I am Grateful for	The Best thing about Today

Things I learned today!

Goals for the day	Action steps to meet goal(s)

Thoughts & Reflections of the day

Daily Journal

I am Grateful for

The Best thing about Today

Things I learned today!

Goals for the day

Action steps to meet goal(s)

Thoughts & Reflections of the day

Daily Journal

I am Grateful for

The Best thing about Today

Things I learned today!

Goals for the day

Action steps to meet goal(s)

Thoughts & Reflections of the day

Wrapping Up!

Self care is extremely important. You can be more effective and you can become more connected with yourself when you practice good self-care. You will be able to handle stress better and you can become more productive in your day and in your relationships. These are just a few of the benefits of effective self care. It is important to re-evaluation your self care levels and needs throughout your life, and make appropriate adjustments in particular, if there are life changes and/or challenges.

You can do this.
You deserve this!
Self care is not selfish!

Made in the USA
Monee, IL
07 July 2026

56685306R00037